LOVELY DREGS

LOVELY DREGS

Richard Sipe

POEMS

atmosphere press

CONTENTS

The Remainder Man

Just Saying, Praise

I Praise Mom and Dad, my Grandfather,
I praise Roberto Clemente, Kurt Vonnegut,
Beethoven, Eminem, Monty Python
Mythology, Mahler, Star Trek
Vito Corleone, Superman,
Martin Espada, and Tom Jones.

I Praise Justin Wilson, Julia Child and Dan Ackroyd.
I praise peanut butter and the Maker's Mark,
George Carlin, Lewis Black, Camel Lights
and saying Fuck whenever I want.

I Praise my Wife, and acceptance,
Lost Causes, because they are lost,
I praise a cat sleeping
on top of a dog's belly
Bittersweet and Gladiolus
bedding down in my garden,

I praise Tolerance whenever...
....Wherever it occurs....
I praise woods I can walk in
Sunsets I can bathe in,
Mysteries I can wash in.

And, I praise the crickets
at night for this skin that I'm in,
a porous takeout container
for the dissonant smoothie inside
with only this lovely,
bendy, straw for air.

FAMILY RESIDUE

Reunion in Beaver Falls

I am from Beaver Falls Pa,
part of Beaver County,
County Seat in the town of Beaver.

And I can tell you straight-on
that in 27 years I never
saw one damned beaver
...the whole time...

But I did see the night lit up
by blast furnaces all along
the Ohio River Boulevard
on the way to Pittsburgh,

I saw my father bent
by 21 turn shifts in a Cold Draw
pulling pipe, I saw
a thick, gray river
run past the Devout College

On the hill where the mill
fires paid for my brains but burned
my soul in cigarette plumes
over a smoker's porch

Where the agnostics hung out
over the Beaver River, where
I gave birth to wanting to leave.

I am from Beaver Falls
where the years snuffed out the mills,
laid off a generation,
and seeded the diaspora of the next,

Where every house on every street

was for sale, wishing to dig itself up,
to redeem its soul from mortgage
and the need to change.

Beaver Falls, Beaver County,
County Seat of Beaver,
where a clean blue river

Flows today by a gas station economy,
and the   one each legacy
donut and pizza shop   still there,

River flowing, falling by me,
stranger on the green bank,
a ghost of quit habits

staring up at the cross on the hill
one bank above the Devout College,
quite the going concern here now,

Hoping for a sign...some portent,
for a blast, for a smoke, for one
God-damned bully beaver.

Breakfast for Dinner

On Tuesdays, we had breakfast for dinner
Mom's French Toast was my sister's favorite

She used whole milk, eggs and
plenty of nutmeg and cinnamon

But her super secrets were the
dry old bread crusts kept in the fridge

just for the soak, her heavy
high walled skillet for frying

and that real A&P maple syrup
for the bubbly margarine top

We sure had our sweet feasts
on Tuesdays back then

the three of us happy green stamps
stuck in a little book

It was a reason to look forward
to Tuesdays every week

Mom made dinner early those nights
so she could take a nice nap after
on the hallway couch

TCC/TES Club, 1985

No one knew what the name
stood for, but it turned out to be

the largest known sado-masochistic
sex club in Pennsylvania,

and it was busted in downtown
Beaver Falls at Morrell's
Family Restaurant.

The Dungeon Room on the second floor
was poised over the kitchen,
right above the pastitsio special

and fluffy cream pies we always had
for Sunday repast after church.

I remember watching the Centennial parade
from a second story window
of the Brodhead Hotel in 1968.

Morrell's Family Restaurant
was directly across the street,
its own second story at eye level

where the bacchanalians must have relished
their own pomp and circumstance that day,

all whipped, trussed and drizzled
behind picnic gingham curtains,

right across from me and up
from the pageant river floating by,

a century's celebration of tradition and faith
in meatloaf and meringue.

Yellow Belly

At six years old he watches his father
      Waving goodbye

As the Checker pulls away from the curb
      Rescued family in tow

Later staying at Grandads
        no one says a thing about it

But he knows it's his fault

Had to be had to be Had To Be
        That's why the quiet polite

Constipation   the occupation
        When there's only shit to tell

The true story was promised once
        But they all would sooner die than tell

So guilt gnaws a craw
        Aims the body down a river

Bumpity bumpity bump bump...
        The delecti   floats

By former homes
        Where once he posed inside a frame

Bumpity bump through former flames
        And self-distilling prophecies

To a bar where he sits
        Affably, laughably regaling

His soon to be 4th wife
	With his yellow jitney tale

"So tell me", she asks, imagining his father's wave...
	"How did that fuck you up?"

Tarantella

At Catalano's Fruit Stand
in Pittsburgh's Strip District
you could bet that every banana crate
shipped over with a tarantula or two
on board, the size and spread
of a child's hand.

And yet, with such a common
hazard along for the ride
no one heard of a bite
or poisoning croak in years.

So when Frank, the stand's purveyor,
got stung it made the front page
of the Post-Gazette
that day in 1938.

His swollen arm was the
featured *corpus delecti* on the foil...
but no real evidence proves the fatality
of a tarantula bite

It is only a mild venom, after all
drawn to allergy
or so the Science tells us
but if you're worried

after the chomp
you can dance
that's where the *tarantella* comes from
...or... you could simply scream..

Salisbury Acres

In 1968 I learned about the 17 year cicadas
when they celebrated their ritual
rising from the ground, shedding their shells

seeking the height of apple limbs
to spread parchment wings,
and lumber off to revel in the fields.

They were red eyed, fat, and docile,
But when I tossed one into my sister's hair
she screamed and ran away in a flurry.

I remember my grandfather sweeping
them off tree trunks at his Pennsylvania farm
where they whirred in deep lit summer woods all night.

In '85 my grandfather died, but not before
I returned home that Spring to cicada song,
to the welcome tymbals in the timber,

the farm overrun with rust and riot,
no brooms in sight, the celebrants dropped
on my shoulders, and told me I had changed.

*I don't get 17 years of sleep between jobs
like you,* I said...*It's fairly relentless above ground,
and there's more to life than love and sex....*

In '02 the farm had gone suburban...Salisbury Acres,
and the patio cookout crowd
flailed at the bug-eyed buggers with spatulas and tongs

and I no longer cared what the beasties thought of me.
But their lives lived underground for so long
I never forgot...sometimes dreamed about

Wouldn't you sing in chorus trees
After sixteen years and 47 weeks under the dirt
Would you not fly and fuck, and stay up all night?

Wake up the neighborhood with your raucous music
Make them call the cops and try to find you
Because you are Everywhere...

Next cycle, if I am alive...and still here,
I will send a birthday card
to Salisbury Acres,

addressed to the ground
          where they will surface   with me...
some coming summer,
perhaps, my last locust plague.

Near Perfect Certainty

You sneak up behind me
in these well-roamed
 isles and racks,

brush your hands over my eyes,
And the rustle of your

breath in my ear whispers
"Guess Who?"

I look around,
but you're never there.

....must be the muzak's incipient sales ghost
planting unbidden suggestions

Closing time and people
make for the exit as evening

coils down the ramps
and winds the way to home

to sit across from each other
at their tables
in near perfect
certainty.

splitting hostas

we divided the hostas

every spring

before they exploded

in variegated clouds

mushrooming our beds

we drove fresh spades

ground thin and keen

into their hearts

hollowed out holes

for the prophylactic good

of the coif

at evening we peeled off

our hands   supped

on the deck

over the preen

and slept on a queens quilt top

bookended spines

split perfectly

over   white

cotton mulch

Ex Ties

An old tie of mine
is buried around the neck

Of my former father-in-law
        nice guy

Good Ford salesman
mall walker after the bypass

But there was no cravat
to go with his suit when he passed

And I had this worn maroon
 dotted silk in my bag

bobble scarfed by
failed presentations

It really powered up his post-pinstripes
and so down he went
and still he is

With my chin oil around his neck
beyond the ferment now
both of us getting used to the underneath

They don't remember this—
the family   former   and who

keeps track of this shit
above ground   anyway
 in the time travels of tense

designations and appellations
where the "is's" and the "are's"

dissolve every second

into a sweet tea that was,
when "ex" is still a tie

that binds, though a knot
unraveled long ago.

A Thankless Giving

My ex-wife's family--
        Now they knew
                How to hold a grudge

 Mean old ladies
        Huddled around
                Thankless Giving's

Carving and Spatching away at each other...
        But the worst
                Was the Silent Treatment

And the Death Bed
        Was no excuse for idle Forgiveness Talk
                Or conciliation
        Chatter

One time, in fact
        A Nearly Swooned sister
                Conjured her twin approaching
                        The Pearled Gates seeking
Welcome

St Peter saw this in Process
        Asked her what to do
                And she said
                        Tell her I went to Hell

We know this dream came true   because
        They both appeared to us Much Later
                The Twins   one Thankless Giving

                All Booed-up and Opaque
        In the middle of Pie
Just to let us know

They get along Swell now

And also   for us
        to not be so   afraid of Hell
                Because all the down training here
                        Really Helped.

Kansas

I think I'll go to Kansas

when the war is over.

I've heard of great

green plains in Kansas,

the pensive corn

stretching on for days,

and those crucifix

roads carved across the wheat,

exhaling redemption,

doom, or benign oblivion

down any swath, and

over the sweet compass air.

The Agnostic on Christmas Eve

The wretched equivocator sleets up
 at the end of O Holy Night.

He's a sucker for those high notes....
overwrought...just like opera.

But his secular window decking
delivers him to some sort of spirit
as the big night approaches

That's when a glimmer comes over
his headboard pane

Actually it's one of those cordless
resin candles he's duct-taped to the sill,

the kind with the new Santa Cell
alkalines, miraculous and abiding
for the long sleepers

He has them in every window during the season
and on Christmas Eve he likes
to leave them on.

That one in his bedroom window is a blinker
and keeps him up all night.

Elm Grove Cemetery
Mystic, CT

I plotted here in this spot
next to the river

had a stone carved
with my name on it

then scattered upon
some untenanted wind

But this spot by the Mystic
will always be mine

nestled down with
my fellow formers.

Casual acquaintances
ambling by

might not recall
my demise

as they muse upon my
chiseled span

that faux, fancied date
on the right having been

one Hell
off a deep breath.

Down Tote Road

In the mogul wreckage wake of a Sugarloaf
weekend, careening and flailing over stumps,

I would head back, the Maine-line,
South 27 through drifted shires.

And come the bend into Belgrade Lake
there was a shop sign on the right

that proffered a singular place
they called the Wisdom Center.

And I would slow the truck in passing,
my brood all a snooze around me,

to scoff and guffaw at the New Age Pabulum,
cheer a Sumatra Dark Toast to the flag

then hammer down on my hell bent,
Super-Sized, Big Gulp grind for home.

Today, the store is shuttered
after flirting with a few other shingles,

and I quit skiing five years ago, caved
to broken ribs, and a nose for gravity.

I still go the Loaf for the kids, but no need
to slow on Belgrade Bend anymore.

Even so, as I ponder slipping away
those downhill days from

the Wisdom Center, up creeps a certain
twitch... a secret itch that I might have

Stopped...just...one... time
along the way,

Parked at the Wisdom Center
stepped up to the counter
and ordered a Large.

The Island

You've got to like bleak
on Orr's Island in Maine,
because it winters here for six
months before a mud grey spring
launches sail boat races obliquely
into the late June wind.

They say *saasage* and *paak* out here
where the alphabet is AAAAAbc
where wild turkeys are the Island Bird
once nearly extinct, now head-strutting
in parade over their own crosswalks
on the only island road in and out.

Did you know that Maine
is demographically the oldest state
in the country? And that Orr's
is part of the most venerable town
in the most geezerly state
from sea to shining sea?
It's a pleasure to decay here
because there's always more rings
around the next tree.

The KKK came out to Orr's in 1924
and posed for pix at the Fourth of July cookout.
They left the next year but not before sixty
per cent of the Islanders had thrown on the sheets
against the Irish and French Canadians.
There is a photo of that picnic
displayed at the Orr's Island Library,
and if you were to ask why it was there
they would tell you "Lest we forget",
which is good, but reticence can whip up a storm itself,
so eventually they posted a plaque to explain.

Reticence, by the way, is the Official Dialect of the island.

And speaking of storms, the chainsaws roar out here
after Nor'easters blow the crows from the birch.
There are hymn sings on Sundays,
lobster bakes by the cove

and a four day fireman's auction in August--
the bulliest fund-raising fest of the year
where if you wait to the last day
you can cop a whole sack
full of crap for fifty cents.

I've copped a few sacks in my time
and hid them from my wife.
She is not into crap, but I will tell you
that her renovated family cottage
is wicked near perfect,
where we live out here on the Island,
where you need an excuse to go into town.

And the Blessing of the Fleet
at our potluck yacht club
is annual and devout
And the vesper bells ring,
the white rose wreaths slip
into the ice summer water,
and then we grill the *saasage* and *paak*,
and then...it's bleak again.

Santino on the Causeway

Her evangelical spleen,

explodes my being

over the causeway,

my poxed carrion

to be eschewed

by the morally

upright buzzards

shunning off

all a-squawk

in search of more

redeemable kill.

Skeleton Key

The key falls from
your father's old desk,
right in front of you,
clangs on the hard
red pine floor
by your feet, and is gone.

Not even the track light
belly beaming under registers
and curtain drop can find it.

Indicting the cat doesn't help...
and if she knew, she would still be
indisposed to confession

So there must be something
in his desk
he doesn't want you
to find...

But that's unlikely
after all this time
and many
thorough
cleanings...

So it's all your stuff
inside there now   right?
And your own wicked
skeleton key

At large among us
conspiring
with the splinters and clips
and a fuzzy cough drop
somewhere.

Soap Wish

I would
  reincarnate myself
        as a sentient
bar of soap
  against your
   skin
sliding along
  your overs
        unders   and
in-betweens
  the crescent
        scar
by your spine
  that no one
        can see
the steam
  behind the silk
        leaving my
scent on you
  all day
        while I sit
in a dish
        awaiting
your return.

Muskie Days

Muskellunge   Muskie
        Prized Pike of the Ohio, and Allegheny,
Rock Star of Chautauqua Lake
            where my father angled
            for the strapping, long jawed
acrobats in turbid summer waters.
    He was a traffic manager at a steel mill
            who taught his adopted son how to catch blue gills
and shun the looming Tree Bass
                    near shoreline at pay lakes.

But the Muskellunge
            was Ishmael's alone
              and that finned sinewed devil,
that trembling end of rod, arc, and line
          would yank his poxed fanatic's soul
                    up and down those roiling lakes,

  ...Or so I was never told...
            He was a Depression man who kept soap slivers
in a Folgers can   cash   in the lettuce crisper
            polished his shoes with black wax
and a horsehair brush   a lover of winter
            for the good drinking water in cold pipes,

But his proud
            fought out   empty hands
                  brought back home to us
            those sweet Musky days,
              the clean, unburdened end
              of his spear.

The Wishing Well

There were wild flowers in the yard,
and I picked them for my mother
one day when I was a kid.

She was delighted with the blooms,
and put them in a jelly jar,
filled with water, atop the kitchen counter.

But...kids being kids...later that day, in some
forgotten tantrum, over some unsated wish,
I snatched the bouquet from the glass,
and scattered it off the porch.

When I came back from the hurl,
she had put the jar away, and was humming
over Tuna Noodle Casserole—a specialty of hers,
and a favorite around our Formica fold.

I've had many wishes since that time,
and One is always to will those flowers
back from the toss, to redeem them away

from my conditional, collateral affection,
and win back her indulgent smile
and my own blissful ignorance
over a bunch of dandelions.

But...old is old now,
acts define a moment,
moments pile up to a life,
and wishes are for wells.

I still pick weeds sometimes
perhaps too often,

gentle bouquets of mistakes
atop my mantle spread, but today
no child is forgiven.

In Kind

In hotel rooms where

mirrors creep up

in sodden places

I see my grandfather

walking across the floor

I recognize the rigid shuffle

and stern bent forward

aimed for the frequent destiny

of the "can"

He was a hard man to like

became more like himself

the older he got

but worth a toast I think

a gesture he never refuses

to return in kind

RUBBLE OF LOVE

Remembering Gethsemane

I am shit-faced and pissing
in my driveway
beneath a gaggle of stars.

Jesus never needed to do this.
That is what knowing all
the answers will do for you.

It will keep you from weaving
the midnight winkle
pondering gravel and grace.

The stars...the inscrutable stars
withhold their sense of all this,
they wink back at me,

remembering Gethsemane
like it was yesterday, wondering
if I will ever be forgiven.

Perennial Mayhem

The garden is not for delicate dispositions
distressed to watch humping

beetles on the weeping cheery,
not for the squeamish, who shrink

from the chomping rot,
gorging on variegated junipers

You there...we need more Preen and Ortho
over by the pussy willows

to muffle the sorrel and cockleburs
molesting Iris and Dahlia by the rock wall.

The Roses are unable to grapple with this,
and try choking themselves with milkweed

This garden is a war zone, deer coleslaw,
and we stewards, pay feckless witness

to fornication, gluttony and murder
between the clean, sculpted stone edges,

there the poor perennial spoil, roils
in the ant hills, grubs in sodden mayhem,

waves madly for sanctuary
at the distant kitchen window.

Curb Weeds

In early June, curb weeds crack
through the seams in sidewalks, and break for the sun.

You see them on the Interstates, sprung
from Jersey Barriers, dropping trow,
waving in ragged abandon at the traffic.

Along my evening walk by the tracks
they scratch at my shins from the knee wall
and fence, some waist high: reedy
fun house ghouls, leering stalkers out for
a belch in the breeze,
seedy flashers flaunting themselves before
the coiffed hostas across the street
in their manicured beds.

About Labor Day, the Town Roadies come down
with their wackers and Zambonis
and they sweep the streets of the lovely dregs
now parched brown with drought, all partied out.

I walk the clean concrete of Autumn unmolested,
the bacchanalia of the weeds blowing in my ear,
unbidden, like murky, sweet bar memories
rising from the mist,
punching the juke with another tune,
playing with the scraping counterpoint of rakes.

Fear and Trembling
at the Bottle Redemption Center

The old attendant heard a buzz and clatter
From the bottle machines outside
opened the upper window of his service door to find
the distraught sophist he knew so well
all puffed and collared in his century's garb
molesting one of the plastic crunchers.

"Problem, sir?" the caretaker inquired,
"Only the supreme hypocrisy
of Redemption proffered here,"
wailed Kierkegaard.
"I have breached a great distance
coming to this place, to offer
my barren, empty vessels in fervent Hope,
only to have them devoured
before me with no regard,
save for this infernal droning."

"Be patient" the old man answered
in a gentle and resonant tone,
"We aren't perfect here, you know."
With that, he produced a singular key
and muted the moaning bottle muncher
with the simple authority
of a click.

"Here you are, sir"

Kierkegaard glared down despairingly
at the paper slip in his hand.
"You call this redemption?" he cried
"We call it a voucher" the
caretaker replied, "Just go in there
 and claim your reward."

The window closed then,
and Kierkegaard gazed across
the courtyard; watched the wide,
glass doors parting   parting
by themselves; beheld the clean
white   light and aproned angels inside
and contemplated another
leap   of   Faith.

Old Tee Shirt

The older I get, the less I seem to care

About things like topical tee shirts

You know...the ones that say you've been someplace

Like this one that says "Dallas"

To be honest, I've never been to "Dallas"

But I sure as hell got the shirt

Picked it up on a layover to somewhere Out West

Here's another tee: Newport, Rhode Island

Now...I've actually been there

Showed up seventy years late to the Gilded Bash

But just in time for the Big Cup Closeout sale in '83

Truth is the world doesn't give a rat's ass

Where you've been...Cares only

About what's rubbed off under the cotton

This is a good one at bottom of the drawer:

 "The Dirty Drummer, Phoenix, Arizona"

That was a chicken wing dive as I recall

I remember the fry cook setting his burgers

On fire over an open flame with a long pour

Of cheap red wine

Which I tried once at home

And would not recommend.

Back Scratcher

I love a good back scratcher--
those telescopic reachers

that sink way down to the smalls
They're $3.99 at CVS

so you can leave them
everywhere for cheap

The one by my nightstand
has an evil, pocked look

with swollen knuckles
and honed talons

It's the perfect scrape
against those unbidden

itches
in the pitch

Benny's Home Stores Closing

All of the Benny's,
some 31 Home Stores
in three states,
closed at the end of last year.

And with them went
715 red-vested souls who knew
Where   Stuff   Was.

And while my humble mouse
can click and scratch
its virtual way through
a cyber hardware maze,

When an actual
Finger points
to the actual widget
I need to carry on,

Well...that is
Sistine Retail
in my chapter
 and verse...

Trans-substantial deliverance,
to the checkout lane
with the perfect
bag of screws.

Bully Congregation

The lily pond croaks by

the former Baptist Church,

its muffled steeple stretching to the blue

while the bull frogs below belch out

praise for the sun on their backs.

God rents this house,

now devoid of flock and tithe,

to an office construction company

who has altered its mission

for profit and partitions.

It pays the bills, while His true tenets,

offer alms to the water by the woods,

free from the stiff, unforgiving pews,

they exult upon their pads

in the magic muck and weeds.

Distant Edge of an Orchard

Each year Hemmings Motor News
publishes a calendar of ascetically
abandoned automobiles

Vintage Galaxies, and Golden Hawks
driven out into the wheat,
by a forest creek
where they revel each month
in the gypsy moss shedding rot
seized up in the joints.

One of them—this August's Nash—
has a tree trunk growing up through its nose

Many of these husks were dreams once
like the finned '57 T-Bird oxidizing blue
by the pond weeds
Or the family aspirational '49 Buick Super
snowed-in up to its portholes

But the '64 Impala shedding vinyl
behind the yellow barn promises reclamation
to celebrants of the mechanically inclined

While I schedule my life into the little white
boxes beneath those deciduous hulks
Urology, Root Canals, blood labs
knee tunes and boil lancing's

all the rattle can primer stuff
that paints over bubbles and rust
and sets old tin lizzie about the block again
low beams trained
on the distant edge of an orchard

Zombie Love Sonnet II

I'd snack on your ears, and not throw them up,
Ravish your liver in savory broth,
Eschew not your eyes, an elegant sup
And munch on your butt with an ardent froth.
But my jaw is partially rotted off
And it's so wrong for the undead to dine
On itself, but gnaw and nibble and quaff
Quicker viscera, less fetid than thine
And whilst you don't have lips and arms or thighs
Your fond torso is much more than so-so,
To this puffer who has suffered awry
From a zorpor with a snowstorm in toe.

   This evening, let's shovel you up some feet
   And dead-walk over to mother's and eat.

Home on the Range

By the time the Ankricks arrived

the smart phones had sucked

all the liquid from our brains

so we didn't see their space ships land

It didn't matter because by then

our neck bones had evolved

to the point we could only look down

and we didn't notice the round up

until the Ankricks were nearly

five years into it.   By that time

we were used to the fences and pens

and friends disappearing around us

from time to   time

every now and then

   the abattoir clamor

Many of us found productive work

writing recipes for ourselves on line

both savory and sweet

some very assertively   gourmet

Only the luckiest among us were able

to get into the best restaurants

It usually came down to the sauce

Dung Beetles

Dung Beetles feed
mostly on dung,

they have the unique ability
to dispose of dung

250 times heavier
than themselves
in a single night,

Sometimes they attach
themselves to dung providers,
just waiting for the dung to occur.

They are seldom disappointed,
while improving

nutrient recycling
and soil structure in the process.

Some are called "Rollers"
molding the dung into round balls

a pound of which they
can push uphill, where they live;

others are known as "Tunnelers"
and they work

to bury the dung
wherever they find it,

and then...there are the "Dwellers",
those who can't roll or bury dung

but become content
to live in it.

Mating Habit of Socks

Socks don't care who
they end up with,

the myriad
matching plains,

swapping partners,
mingling lint

right here
in the laundry

wanton cotton, on top
of the dryer...

with me, pimp sorter,
bundling random two's
into the basket

And so off they are
the swinging
greys and blues

to a nestle
in the dresser,

The blazing
jacquard plaids

magenta
in their envy.

Papule Opus

Dr. Pimplepopper is a well-watched

cable show where various forms

of carbuncles are cut and squeezed to expose the

the urgency of internal matters.

There, the unseemly purulence

erupts into a pure spring release

of gelatinous demons over

our wicked skin.

Throughout, Dr. Pimplepopper

provides professional assurance

that it's OK to enjoy the spectacle

as she sops up another papule opus.

Welcome assurance indeed

for the boil-denier,

Discreetly raptured from PBN

telethons with Rene Fleming

into such delicious guts

a voyeur sofa spud who

wants to watch it

all come out.

Punctuation Confrontation

Not the stern declaration
of the Period
or the insolent catechism
resident in the Question

We need more forbearing
            Punctuation
to quench the slavering fawn
            of the Exclamation

            Point!

Not to impugn the Colon here
and summon unwelcome
            Expectation

But if we spoke more parenthetically
we could mean less of what we say
            (and say it anyway)

Fly in the margin between brackets
a more circumspect conjugation
less rattle
            more Dash--

Science of Pressure

Did you know
there is the atmospheric
pressure of two equivalent
elephants weighing down on you
--right now?

You don't feel it, do you?
That's because the force is being
equally applied in all directions.
That's what the science
of pressure tells us.

Which means that you have
one elephant's ass
in your face—right now--
but it's ok because number two's
left foot is up yours.

This is why you can keep
your car on the road this morning
as you drive to work,

Staying in your lane, though somewhat
equivocally now,
as the world smells
a little different.

Soon Enough

Lady Cat jumps up
on the armchair

stares past my shoulder
to the library door

and the ghost entering
the room

If I looked around this moment
I am sure

there would be no ghost
but there is an image

in the cat's eyes:
some opaque wraith

she has seen
here before

and chose
in her cryptic

cat-ness not to disclose
They must have a deal

the spurious haunt
and she:

Keep the lazy boy
in the dark...

...He will know
soon enough

Summer Bugs

Summer bugs slip

through rents in your screens

rapture around kitchen lamps,

hum up the cabinets

dodging the sour dish rag

snapping from your hand.

In the intimate black

of dank, flung sheets,

they lick high C's in your ears,

and their blood love blooms

again on your shoulders and thighs

after next morning's shower

aflame with welt, ecstatically....

shamefully, scraped by you

with crunchy linen towels.

Troubleshooting Your New Washing Machine

Code	Meaning	Solution
4E	Your washer has tried to fill but was unsuccessful	Check your feet... if they are wet... leave the laundry room.
UE	An Unbalanced Load has prevented your washer from spinning	Try reasoning with it.
dE	After the spinning cycle has completed, your clothes are still wet	Make sure the dryer is working.
dE1	The washer door will not lock after the cycle is complete	You have more underwear somewhere, don't you?
FU	The washer will not respond	How is that Extended Warranty looking to you now?
HA	Your claim has been denied	We look forward to serving you in the future.

Writing a Poem like Billy Collins

I am going to sit
in this breakfast nook
and write a poem like Billy Collins
You can watch me   quietly.

It is very early in the morning
so my drink still has ice in it.
Someone spilled the salt and pepper
all over the red gingham

and no one has noticed but me
the incidental harmony
of brine and kick in this mix
against their grains

The cat is perched on a granite stoop
by the gaping slider, heading out
for the morning when I recall that she
is an indoor cat, declawed like a clay pigeon

pursued by me into the rich black mulch
over cragged Hydrangea rocks
to a tripping, flat back sprained
view of the waking sun.

My wife has stirred from sleep
to this picture-potted frame of a new day
and I wonder if we have become
friends after all this time.

Go ahead, have a pear with thick
whole grain toast and cream,
lean in the doorway and wish this was you
writing this   listen

to the vesper hornet hum,
the opera sirens wailing high C's
through closer roads and hills,
the scour of a sandpaper tongue,
a distant purring overhead.

The Cough

A good cough knows
        when night is falling

And a bad cough
        knows it better

It's easier during the day

when you're walking upright
        for everything
to quag out

But prone
        in the gloaming
with the coal closing in

That's when the true hack
        sits up
on the cold corner

of a pit sectional
in the basement

escapes to the attic
        sand bags overcome

schmuck stuck to the roof

trying to heave it all up
        under the wry night

Young Flaming Romantic

Keats's urn beneath those happy boughs
wrought curses upon the nascent
romantic and his ethereal concept of loins.

So the strapping Poe,
flung thence forth
on a midnight deep and dreary
with a crow on his back

to froth upon the moors,
to seek actual, tangible loins
upon those heath fring'd legend haunts.

But that brooding "Nevermore"
soot, cawing fowl clawed
a crapping pox upon his sleeve,
and continued to excrete pessimism

upon his peat,
now marsh mired,
until the potted maidens,
overwrought,
whispered on about soft pipes...

...which happens now and then
behind the Chamber Doors.

THE REMAINDER MAN

Squander

Something about a Q
in any word wonders
what it's about

Quandary at the bend
qualm in a hunch
or quince in your pie,
It's always
the quarterback's fault
for the quirk

And after the squall
we all have doubts
--squash or gourd—
you never know
what the squid inks up
in the quiet of the quilt,
the quixotic scribble
of the sheet

Squander is a good
word too
It sounds like something
it has to do
 and it rhymes
with Ponder which
has no Q.

The Last Fireworks

I don't care if

I see another

Fireworks display

The first one

I had to myself

And it cracked

  Up my sky

The rest

Are only

sequels

With traffic

Drinking Boat

A River Styx
runs between us

And you are on
the quick side

And I am waving
from a drinking boat

Tethered to a dock
and you think

I have a boat
but I do not

bagged

potato chip morsels

intense slippery

sour cream smidgens

salty bottom

bag dregs

why should a poem

at midnight

exist

about them

those savory

iambic iotas

sliding from

a fingers tweeze

counting both

as sustenance

and sin

Farmer's Market, Westfield New York

The raven haired

Amish girl behind

the checkered red table

takes a break to eat

a sure slice

of country bread

and heirloom

tomato steak

cut thick and lush,

open face in the sun,

her upturned palm

like a plate

Sonny's Town and Country Restaurant and Motel, Three Nights Before Christmas

The Juke box wails at the maudlin command of my quarters
and the snow piles up outside this blizzard afternoon.

Blizzard afternoon with you in this season of naked truth
and Johnny Mathis, and shot glass markers in queue.

We invest in each other's past, and I can almost see you
without your pants, but that might come off later, I hope.

Later, is drive time and the blizzard flies over flat screens
and traffic is daft, but Perry Como is home for the holidays
and so are we.

Home. I scarcely know you now, but I knew
you would come out in a storm like this

to watch the lights blink around the Miller Lite clock
as if it were your own hearth.

The storm makes it better, and the affinity for Christmas
fogs our glasses as I watch your ass head off for the can.

There is a motel here, but not enough currency to spend the
night.
So I think about us doing it right here in my car,
Like we did that one time I'm surprised to remember

That one time, when I didn't drop my keys in the snow,
Which is heavy and wet in your hair, your cold black hair
in the backseat.

In the back seat a tin Andy Williams sings O Holy Night
as you straddle my lap and we look up through a skylight
frozen open.

Used Book

Just inside the dog-eared flap,
his inscription read
"Property of Jeff Pritchard",

scribed in ink, no less,
the fluid of permanence,
a Great Walled scrawl

meant to thwart such renegade
book annexing bastards
as me in my spine cracking tracks.

"No, no", I recoiled, in a stroke
of succession and plunged my quill
to the title page

"Mine Now! All Mine Forever...Mine!"
I slashed my seal across the leaf;

a very vervey flag-plant on my part, to which
Mr. Pritchard has yet to respond.

Jesus...not another pissing in the dark poem

The best poem I ever wrote
about pissing outdoors
at night

was the one with Jesus
in it...well...

Jesus wasn't
exactly
in the poem

But he did make
an appearance
by reference

and provided
the necessary
epiphanic link
between ignorance
and forgiveness

which all
pissing in the dark
poems should strive
to do

The Methodist Chu...

That Which is Unacceptable
is Merely Something that You
Haven't Gotten Used to Yet
            ---Anonymous

The permanent shutdown
was made a lesser ado
by knowing we would be fed.

And the EZ-to-Follow instructions
on how best to screw a flap
into our front doors for the trays

to pass through were quite helpful,
at a time in the home when
we all needed something to do.

And some of the burgoos
that came scooting under
the skirt were quite savory,

though not scooting thru as often
as we would like, but, hey, it is true,
they say, we could all eschew

a few meals for our collective health.
And because, later, there was no
power, the firewood was a boon;

Some branches, logs and twigs, but mostly
boards and siding from buildings
not required in the new. In fact

one particular plank that threw beneath
my flap one night said "Methodist Chu"
in faded red lettering, the last letters

being near the edge of a ragged cut
which made a nice crackle going up the flue
as the stew sizzled succulently over the "Chu",

where I remember belonging once,
and wondered how they knew.

Piranha Tank

I don't remember much from 1962
being only six, but I can still
conjure the Cuban Missile Crisis
from the stool next

To my stepfather's chair, his hand
on my back, reassuringly,
as we watched the young President
on our Magnavox console.

There were missiles and bases
and bombers just off the coast,
and I've read about them since,
listened with a grown-up ear
to Kennedy's warnings,
only to return to the security
of the hand on my back.

Eleven months later, that young
president was murdered by a man
I later saw shot right in front of me
as the cameras rolled.

And the world was a funeral
pyre for a week after
as my mother hooked
a harvest rug in the dining room
and the dirges wailed on the screen.

I've later read theories, seen movies about
the assassination, none of which
take me far away from
that dining room and the calm
latching and looping of yarn
through stiff burlap backing.

That rug ended up
in my sister's house
in a spare bedroom
patching the pocked floor in front
of her piranha tank,
where I slept, or tried to,
when visiting;

Where that toothy,
vigilant little beastie--
only one among the disparate
and magical brood of life forms
that she hosted there—
would stare me down as if I were
a roast.

Momen

Momen was a nickname for "moment "
in his unbridled rookie days...
"Momen...Momen",

take a minute to look at the pitch
before swinging
from that cocked stance

where even a whiffed strike
blew the air out of Forbes Field;
Momen, leaping into the ivy

off right field wall for the stab
always twisting your
neck from the crashes.

Captions like "hypochondriac"
"complainer" and "malingerer"
peppered the sport pages then,

But you, Momen, shed that skin
gunned down those runners
at home with a blow

from your Pirate's cannon arm
They're not going home, Momen
much like you on that rattletrap,

overburdened DC7, a bad pitch
you chased with an urgent purpose
on New Year's Eve 1972

to fly relief supplies
to quake victims in Nicaragua.
You had to make that trip yourself

because no corrupt bureaucrat would dare
snatch comfort from a child's hand
with the great Clemente on the watch.

But who am I to say? Certainly not
a native of Puerto Rico, but I am
blood to the Pittsburgh kids of the 60's,

we selfish homer fans who wished
that you had not plunged
into that moment for others

so selfish of you not to think of us
Saint Momen of the Moment
You could not have contemplated

how many so many of us still steeped
in that vintage must turn away a mist,
even now, when we hear your name.

> *If you have a chance to accomplish*
> *something that will make things better*
> *for people coming behind you,*
> *and you don't do it,*
> *then you are wasting your time*
> *on this earth.*
> *--Roberto Clemente*

Old Tee 2

It's hard to give up on

      an old tee-shirt

So much of your hidden self has

      rubbed off under it

that a Good Will Store

      might spill your secrets

And there you go

      down the street

 husk of the nut

      you once were

a bonafide kernel

      without the squirrel

a ranting sandwich board

      without the ham

trying to explain

      your threadbare self

      to strangers.

Taking a Break from Being a Fish

It floats in the calm
 this lakefront morning,
  on top of the world for a change,
   savoring its first look at the sky.

   Ducks dive, a few docks over...
    down and up, down and up,
     hard at work for breakfast,
      unlike our chum, who already ate,
       now basking, unswimmingly,
        altogether forgetful of being a fish,

         heading for the shore now
          to take a load off, unweight
           from the fish trappings of the undertow
           from fin, scale and gill
           and lap up over a bed of sand
             buy tickets to a new moon watch
              and stare down the sun until dark.

Last Things You Do Before Winter

A calm of stone fences
          runs along back roads
over Maine and up further North

          lost boundaries
                    forested farms
rock resolves   gone to grass
          abandoned to drift and pile

          So...you get ready

swath the lawn short
          crew cut the perennial brood
and rubber mallet down
          your
                    tall
                              reflectors

along the plow borders
          as if to dissuade
                    the blades

Old Superman

I am
	flying
		lower

these days
	the green rock
		being everywhere,

there is even an Ugly
	Christmas sweater

with my logo on it
	but I am
		the only one

here in the Bus Station
	wearing the original copy,

				flying low

	so nobody knows.

Rhapsody in Last Minute Time

*(largely spawned from Queen
and David Bowie)*

[*um ba ba be*] I need to go to bed soon
but I can't sleep, between the dreams

[*dee da day da*] I get to ponder
all through the light [*ee da*]

waiting for our dance at night
[*um ba ba bo*]

You, coifed like a queen
Poised, while sweaty me

[*ee da ee da*] digs a way at a day,
humidly aware

that I can barely clean up
for you in time [*be da dee da*]

to make the bed, under pressure,
hoping some stroke

of luck [*be da dee da dee da dee da*]
chases the tune, with lime,

and one more chance to slide
under your unsuspecting door

[*ba da bee ba*]

Formerly Ed's Chicken

If you find yourself
beginning a poem
with "life" or "love",
you may be writing
a shitty poem.

So change the subject,
bring in Kierkegaard, or better
yet, a Recipe;

But not your Mother's
Veal Birds or Barbie Cups,
for God's sake,

 ...maybe something like that Killer
Chicken recipe you stole from
your brother-in-law, Ed
that one time
when he wasn't looking.

Now that was a keeper.

He conjured and forgot it
both at the same moment,
but you wrote it down
and chefed it up for years.

In fact, it's become your secret sauce,
and everybody loves you for it.

Once, you even fed it back
to Ed himself,
and he loved it so much
he asked you
for the recipe.

See how that works?
Life
	Love
		A Poem
Perfect symmetry
with a killer recipe for chicken
all on a single sheet,

Just don't skimp
on the Liquid Smoke.

And   now,
in the interest of fine poultry,
and all good measure,
	before you expect it...
	here comes
the Inscrutable

End

ABOUT ATMOSPHERE PRESS

Atmosphere Press is an independent, full-service publisher for excellent books in all genres and for all audiences. Learn more about what we do at atmospherepress.com.

We encourage you to check out some of Atmosphere's latest releases, which are available at Amazon.com and via order from your local bookstore:

In the Cloakroom of Proper Musings, a lyric narrative by Kristina Moriconi

Lucid_Malware.zip, poetry by Dylan Sonderman

The Unordering of Days, poetry by Jessica Palmer

It's Not About You, poetry by Daniel Casey

A Dream of Wide Water, poetry by Sharon Whitehill

Radical Dances of the Ferocious Kind, poetry by Tina Tru

The Woods Hold Us, poetry by Makani Speier-Brito

My Cemetery Friends: A Garden of Encounters at Mount Saint Mary in Queens, New York, nonfiction and poetry by Vincent J. Tomeo

Report from the Sea of Moisture, poetry by Stuart Jay Silverman

The Enemy of Everything, poetry by Michael Jones

The Stargazers, poetry by James McKee

The Pretend Life, poetry by Michelle Brooks

Minnesota and Other Poems, poetry by Daniel N. Nelson

ABOUT THE AUTHOR

Richard Sipe lives on Orr's Island in Maine. Originally from Western Pennsylvania, he worked in the shipbuilding industry in Connecticut and Rhode Island for over 35 years. He is a poetry editor, and the audio editor for *The Café Review*, an art and poetry quarterly out of Portland, Maine. His work has appeared in numerous journals. In the winter he likes to shovel the snow off his lawn. "It's a lot of work," he once said, "but sometimes I think it's worth it."

FORMERLY ED'S CHICKEN

2 Pounds Boneless Chicken Breasts
Marinade:
--1/2 cup ranch dressing
--1 T Worcestershire sauce
--1 t minced garlic
--1/4 cup soy sauce
--a couple of dashes of liquid smoke
--a couple of dashes of Maggi seasoning

- Between two sheets of plastic wrap, pound out chicken breasts to about ½ inch thick. Perforate chicken with a knife point to further tenderize.
- Mix marinade ingredients
- In a Ziplock freezer bag, add chicken and marinade. Close bag, and squish well with your hands to mix well.
- Refrigerate for 2-4 hours.
- Heat grill, or oiled grill pan over medium-high heat.
- Grill chicken on each side 3 to 4 minutes on each side, or until cooked through.
- Serve hot off the grill or grill pan.

Note—makes a nice Chicken Caesar Salad: Serve over Chopped Romaine, Parmesan, Salt and Pepper, and Croutons, tossed. Put chicken on top. Serve.